The Caregiver's Path
to FREEDOM

The Caregiver's Path
to FREEDOM

SIMPLIFY YOUR HOME, EASE YOUR STRESS, AND TAKE BACK YOUR LIFE

REBECCA HARTMAN

Library of Congress Control Number: 2024921782

ISBN: 979-8-9986945-1-6   (Paperback)

Printed in the United States of America

Dedication

To my son:

Being your mom is my greatest joy, privilege, and honor.
I love you always.

To Caregivers:
To all the caregivers who show up day after day to give
love and support to the people in their lives, their
community, and work. You are loved and appreciated,
even though it is often unspoken.

Table of Contents

About the Author

Rebecca Hartman earned a Bachelor of Science in Landscape Architecture (BSLA), College of Engineering at The Ohio State University. She worked in the landscape design-build industry for many years, meeting with clients to assess their needs, designing the project, creating proposals, and overseeing the project installation. Projects ranged from simple planting plans to elaborate decks, patios, swimming pool areas, and development of commercial sites.

She later used her design experience to upgrade home interiors. She designed and oversaw remodeling projects for kitchens, bathrooms, whole home lighting, room layouts, flooring, wall color, storage, and more. She also staged a home that sold within 48 hours at the asking price.

Rebecca is a mother and wife. In recent years, she became the caregiver of her mother and quickly realized there is a real need to support women in the sandwich generation. She began writing *The Caregiver's Path to Freedom* to help caregivers cope with the never-ending demands on their time and energy. Her book offers readers hope, reassurance, and solutions for home and life management.

As a caregiver herself, she created this book, its instructions, plans, and to-do lists, knowing caregivers are incredibly overwhelmed and need simple, effective, time-saving solutions.

She enjoys spending time with family and friends. She also enjoys travel, nature, art, animals, hiking, horseback riding, and white water rafting.

Foreword

As a retired civil litigation attorney, I suffer from the addiction common to many of my peers: too much paper. When I learned that Rebecca Hartman, my dear friend and one of the most organized people I know, was writing an organizing guide, I got excited. When she agreed to show me how it could work in my home office, I became positively giddy.

After a short afternoon's shared time (with a lot of laughing and fun), towering piles of unidentified papers became a drawer of alphabetically filed documents, a bag of recyclable paper, and a small bag of shredded private materials. The results seemed miraculous to me but less so to Rebecca, who apparently sees this all the time. "What's important is a system that makes sense to you, not one that makes sense to me," Rebecca reminded me before she left for the day.

And she has been right. I have gone back into those files many times since that spring afternoon, and I can always find what I'm looking for because the categories make sense to me. Even more, I have been able to build on the structure we set up, finally making my home office work for me!

So fear not: Rebecca's got your back. She can help you work your way through your most stressful messes. Give her the opportunity to change your life.

— Anne Owings Ford

Introduction

Discover what awaits within the pages of this comprehensive book. With a wide range of topics covered in simple, easy-to-follow instructions, it sets itself apart from the rest. From room planning and digital photo organization to filing, expense tracking, kitchen layout design, downsizing, and moving tips, this book provides a wealth of valuable information. You won't need to adhere to any specific method or agenda — just dive in and start benefiting from the practical advice and insights it offers.

The Caregiver's Path to Freedom is the ultimate guide for caregivers looking to bring order to their hectic lives. With easy-to-follow step-by-step instructions and ready-to-go to-do lists, this book is your roadmap to managing tasks and organizing your home with ease. Say goodbye to chaos and hello to harmony as you breathe a sigh of relief, knowing at least your home is organized and under control. Whether you're a seasoned caregiver or just starting, this book is your partner in creating a peaceful and harmonious sanctuary for you and your loved ones. Keep this book within reach for guidance through all of life's events.

Get It In Writing

Printable worksheets are included with your book purchase. Visit https://essentialhomeorganization.com/ to download and print the home organization, downsizing, and moving worksheets in PDF format. Click on the Books header then add the E-Book Organization Worksheets to your cart. Use the discount code WKYNB5FNQ21X at checkout to receive the free instant download. Save the files to your computer and print anytime. The code is available for one use per customer. You must enter your email address for delivery. If you have any difficulty with the code, email info@essentialhomeorganization.com.

You will also find additional caregiver resources and information on the Essential Home Organization website in a wide range of topics. Information is added regularly so be sure to check back frequently.

Preface

Unexpected Events

All of us are hit with unexpected events during our lifetime. I recently joined the sandwich generation, caring for my family while also planning for the care of an older parent. Downsizing and transitioning a parent into assisted living is mentally, emotionally, and physically overwhelming. Where do I start? In an instant, I had to decide what to keep, sell, donate, and move while helping my mother cope with the changes. I also became Power of Attorney, responsible for her financial and medical decisions. Fortunately, my home was already organized. It was often quite dirty then, but it remained functional and neat. This allowed me to care for my family while managing what felt like a thousand things at once, including coping with my own emotions.

Afterward

After my son started high school and my mother was settled into assisted living, I finally had room to breathe. You might think I made great use of my newly opened-up schedule. In a way,

I did. I recovered. I spent countless hours over the first few weeks, mostly staring at the family room walls. I had so little time over two years that I never had the chance to emotionally and mentally process witnessing my mother's decline due to dementia. I didn't have time to cope with losing Hunter, my beloved dog. I didn't have time to deal with a health scare. So I sat. I took the time to come to terms with this difficult time in my life, and then I decided to do something productive with all of these challenging experiences. I decided to help other caregivers who were also drowning. Things will get easier for you eventually. You will get to the other side of this difficult time in your life.

I created Essential Home Organization, LLC because my story is not unique. Many people are being pulled in too many directions with work, family, and aging parents. Rather than having a place to escape and recharge, their homes are centers of endless disorganization and stress because many individuals lack the time or skills to create and maintain order. Many solutions, such as self-help books, blogs, and articles are ridiculously long, incomplete, or force one method of organization on their reader. As a designer, I created comprehensive, efficient, and, most importantly, flexible plans. Because life is busy, sometimes hectic, and often very demanding, I like the "get to the point" approach. The goal is to create order. If everything is tossed into a bin, labeled, and placed on a shelf, you still know where to find it. We all have different needs. How much order is enough? Enough is what makes life easier for you.

Time passes so quickly. I sincerely hope the tools and information within this book help you manage your household more efficiently so you can enjoy more time with your loved ones while also caring for yourself.

Chapter One

DROWNING

___

It Wasn't Always Like This

O nce upon a time, we all started on our own as young adults. Do you remember your first place? More than likely, it was a small apartment with a few pieces of used furniture. You had some clothes, some kitchen utensils, pots, pans, plates, and mismatched glasses. Life was easy, and you were on the go, out with friends, or going to college classes. It was a place to eat, shower, and keep a few possessions. It was easy to clean up, and likely you weren't all that invested in it.

Fast forward to your current life and it likely looks much, much different. You may have unwanted family heirlooms you feel obligated to keep, ten years' worth of clothing in various sizes, and excess items that you bought but never really put to use. Add in the items for each family member, all of their interests, hobbies, and sports, and the mountain of items has grown over the years. We may have had a plan to change our lives, but we likely didn't consider how our home would need to change to meet our needs.

Life Events

Some of the most stressful life events are buying a home, becoming a parent, death or care of a loved one, loss of a job, financial challenges, and a change in relationships such as marriage or divorce. Some events are planned and positive, such as buying a home or getting married. Other times, the events are sudden and unplanned, and we are unprepared. Not only do we have the emotional and mental strain, but frequently, the event also sends shock waves through our homes.

After a change, whether sudden or planned, our day-to-day life has been disrupted. With new responsibilities, work and daily routines are suddenly different. The problem then becomes trying to re-establish a routine with new demands. Creating and maintaining a magazine-quality, clean, perfectly designed, and decorated home is unachievable. It isn't a failure. Most of us are not going to be supermodels or famous movie stars. That doesn't make us less, and it just means we are living our own lives.

Shop Therapy

We all enjoy new things. At some point though, we need to realize the new shiny object is just adding to our cluttered home. My mother loved her things. She loved buying new clothes and books.

Unfortunately, she didn't prioritize the thing she loved the most, which was to travel. It was heartbreaking watching her come to the realization she would never fulfill those dreams. There is a real cost to shopping. What are you giving up? What is the benefit? Do you have a big dream, such as a trip to Hawaii? How could you better use your money? Do you want to save for retirement, a new car, a new home, or a trip to Peru? A few dollars here and ten more over there can add up to lost dreams over twenty years.

Super Hero

Often, we go about our daily work and responsibilities without considering exactly what the big picture looks like. How do you spend your time? Do you consider the cost in terms of time and energy? How many hours are spent on your feet? How many hours are dedicated to the wants, needs, and benefits of others? Unless you have super-human abilities, something is going to give. Use the **My Weekly Responsibilities Worksheet** to calculate the number of hours worked each week for each category. You can also write out the headings and hours on a sheet of paper.

My Weekly Responsibilities Worksheet

Childcare: _____hours/week

- Under age 5
- Before & after-school care
- School activities
- Music, speech lessons
- Sports practice, games
- Social events, activities
- Homeschool & homework

Meals: _____hours/week

- Prep
- Cook
- Serve
- Pack lunches
- Clean-up & dishes

Laundry: _____hours/week

- Clothes
- Bedding
- Dry
- Cleaning
- Ironing

Errands: _____hours/week

- Appointments
- Shopping

Pet Care:_____hours/week

- Feed
- Clean up yard, cages
- Exercise
- Train
- Bathe
- Vet appointments

Budget:_____hours/week

- Pay bills
- Evaluate expenses
- Evaluate savings

Career: _____hours/week

- Hours worked for pay
- Travel to and from work

Elder Care: _____ hours/week

- Bathe, dress, provide care
- Meals
- Finances
- Medical appointments
- Social activities
- Legal
- Home maintenance
- Cleaning- see Home Cleaning
- Laundry- see Laundry hours

Home Cleaning: _____ hours/week

- Vacuum
- Sweep
- Mop
- Dust
- Clean walls
- Clean fridge
- Clean kitchen countertops
- Clean bathroom countertops
- Clean toilets, showers, sinks
- Clean windows, mirrors
- Clean garage
- Clean basement
- Straighten and put things away
- Look for lost items

Total of all hours worked:_____

Self-care Hours: _____

- Exercise
- Meditation
- Relaxation
- Hobbies, friends, etc.
- Date night
- Days off, vacation, sick time
- Sleep, relax, rest

When was the last time you:

- Flew a kite
- Went on a picnic
- Rode a horse
- Rode a bike
- Went on a hike
- Walked on the beach
- Enjoyed the sunset
- Enjoyed your favorite hobby or activity
- Felt appreciated
- Felt wanted and loved
- Felt happy

Where is the joy in endless chores, demands, and work? How much time are you able to spend playing with your children, visiting a friend, or developing your interests?

If you feel like you are drowning in all of the demands on your time and energy, there is no one-size-fits-all approach or magic button. Knowing you are not alone isn't comforting when your kids are screaming, the dog is tearing apart the carpet, and dinner is burning. Realizing you can't do it all is the first step in creating change. Now that you have completed the **My Responsibilities Worksheet**, you not only see how you are spending your hours, but you can show your family why they need to accept more responsibility. It is their obligation to clean up after themselves and help maintain their home. If they don't pitch in without constant battles, consider cutting back on your kid's activities or hiring service providers such as lawn care. Delegating or deleting some of the tasks is the only way you will carve out time for yourself, your relationships, and your health.

Chapter Two

MOMMY TANTRUMS & CAREGIVER BURNOUT

My Story: When Life Happened

We will all remember when the Covid pandemic started and how it impacted our lives. Many of us lost loved ones. Our jobs and income were impacted, school life changed for our children, and our social time disappeared. My experience is certainly not special or unique.

In March 2020, my son began homeschooling. His school created the schedule and lesson plan, so I didn't need to do much other than keep him on track with his homework and make lunch. But, after the next full year at home, it was obvious he wasn't going to be ready for high school since his school wasn't prepared to provide remote education. We switched to an online school, and I was, once again, his teacher. It has been decades since I had

Algebra, and I never had to learn Common Core Algebra. Despite my best attempts, I certainly was not good at teaching this subject.

At the same time, my mother began displaying more symptoms of dementia. Her condition deteriorated quickly, likely due to the isolation. I eventually had to take her car keys from her. This is a conversation we all dread.

In August, my beloved Golden Retriever, Hunter, died suddenly. I had trained him to be a therapy dog and had a very deep bond with him. Watching him work and brighten people's day was pure magic. Their joy was so obvious. Men, women, the young, the old, and even the individuals who were afraid of dogs could not help but get caught up in his warm eyes, calm demeanor, and big, welcoming smile. Some heartbreaks don't go away. You simply get used to them.

By October 2020, it became obvious my mother could no longer care for herself. I had to find assisted living that was both reputable and affordable. That was no small task. I also became her medical and financial Power of Attorney and helped her with finances, her will, and burial decisions. When it was time for her to move, I had to help sort mountains of clothes, shoes, and more.

She certainly was not ready to part with many of her belongings. Finally, I had to arrange her move. Helping my mother through this transition and taking care of all of the responsibilities was enough to do by itself without needing to also maintain my household and homeschool responsibilities.

November arrived with my own health scare. While waiting for additional tests, I kept wondering how I could keep up with everything if I also had to battle cancer. I was already exhausted, depressed, and ready to run away. It wasn't one task or one responsibility. It was the mountain of loss and responsibility that felt unbearable. Fortunately, after weeks of stress, the test results came back negative. Although I was far from healthy after neglecting my own health for a long period, I was extremely grateful I didn't need to battle for my life.

Thankfully, my home was organized before everything hit. During those nine months, it certainly wasn't clean. I didn't have the time to worry about clean windows and floors. I certainly was not at all prepared to take on all of my mom's needs. If you do nothing else with this book, create a 3-ring binder for your aging parent(s) and get prepared. Create a plan. Determine who will provide care. Get the legal documents ready before you need them.

You are one health crisis away from your loved one's world colliding with yours.

Essential Home Organization

I know my life events over the last few years are hardly uncommon. I am not seeking some badge of honor for surviving a difficult time in my life. I certainly did not handle it all with grace. I am sharing my story because all of us tend to think everyone else's life is easier than ours, that we could be doing something better, something more. We could be happier, and prettier, make more money, work more, work less, parent better, and help our aging parents more. Many of us have unattainable expectations of ourselves.

In 2022, my son was off to high school, and my mother was being well cared for in a memory care unit close to my home. I finally had room to breathe. I wanted to help other women struggling to find room in their lives for themselves.

I began making home organization worksheets. Recently, I decided it was time to put things together in one organized presentation. Naturally, life threw a curve ball. As I was trying to meet a deadline, Spencer introduced himself to a skunk at 5:50 am, and my husband and son were sick. What deadline? At least through all the life events, I have learned to be more patient, realistic, focused, and balanced.

This is Spencer. He is an English Springer Spaniel, also known as my 50- pound tornado.

Mommy Tantrums

Frustration, impatience, fatigue, anger, and even losing it are part of life. Kids have tantrums. Your boss will sometimes lose it. Yet, as moms, we are expected to be composed, patient, and nurturing 24/7 without taking a moment for ourselves. When mommy tantrums are occurring more often than you would like, it isn't just impacting you. Your stress and frustration are felt by every member of your household and likely spill into work and other relationships.

Caregiver Burnout

Caregiver burnout is a state of physical, emotional, and mental exhaustion experienced by individuals who provide care for a loved one. It can be a result of the constant demands, stress, and responsibilities associated with caregiving. Caregivers often put the needs of their loved ones above their own, leading to neglect of their own well-being.

Signs of caregiver burnout may include feelings of overwhelming fatigue, irritability, lack of motivation, depression, anxiety, and a sense of isolation. Physical symptoms may include headaches, trouble sleeping, weight fluctuations, and a weakened immune system.

To prevent caregiver burnout, caregivers need to prioritize self-care and seek support from others. This may involve setting boundaries, taking frequent breaks, practicing stress-relief techniques, and seeking professional help when needed.

Caregiver burnout can have serious consequences for both the caregiver and the individual receiving care. Caregivers must recognize the signs of burnout and take proactive steps to address their own well-being.

Stopping the Downhill Slide

I had no time for myself. I survived on coffee and sugar. I cut my hair, gained weight, developed health problems, and continue to suffer from horrible insomnia. Even though I love my family and absolutely cherish being a mom, having little to no time for myself or my goals outside of my family was quite frustrating and depressing. Recently, I took steps to redefine my role and duties within my entire family. This led to better health and better relationships. Everyone was supportive. I wish I had not delayed addressing my needs with them sooner.

If you have been carrying a heavy burden for a long time, it is important to take care of yourself and prioritize your well-being. Drawing boundaries with your family members is a positive step toward asserting your own needs and setting limits on what you can and cannot handle. It's okay to prioritize yourself and your own goals, even while fulfilling your duties to your family.

Remember that self-care is not selfish; it is essential for your overall health and well-being. Taking time for yourself, setting boundaries, and seeking support when needed are all important ways to ensure you can continue to care for others sustainably.

If you are feeling overwhelmed or struggling with problems like insomnia, it may be helpful to seek support from a healthcare professional who can provide guidance and resources to help you manage these challenges. It's okay to ask for help and prioritize your own health and well-being. While it is often difficult to redefine relationships, it becomes necessary if you are overburdened and in mental, physical, and emotional decline.

Chapter Three

GETTING HELP

Finding Solutions

W hen the work load is more than you can handle, get help. If your friends or family are encouraging you to get help, don't try to push through. Something will give. Will it be your health? Will your relationships take a hit? Will you lose your job due to mistakes or missed deadlines?

There is no magic solution that will work for everyone. If you have young children, your needs are different than someone with an eighty-year-old parent living with them. Your community center and Google can provide a huge assortment of local service providers.

The real issue is to determine what will provide the greatest assistance and do so within your budget. If the tasks you need the most help with are unaffordable, look at other solutions. Perhaps weekly house cleaning is too expensive, but lawn service is within your budget.

Start with your budget:

- I have an available budget of $ _____ per week.
- Lawn work: $ _____ per week.
- Child care: $ _____ per week.
- Senior care: $ _____ per week.
- Other: $ _____ per week.

Resources:

- Google search
- Facebook groups
- Caregiver searches
- Care.com
- Hospice
- In-home senior care providers
- Assisted living facilities
- Senior daycare
- Meals on Wheels
- Lawn service companies
- Cleaning service companies
- Painting or repairman services
- Home organizing services
- Homeschool communities

Try to think of ways to free up your time. By cutting down on unnecessary activities while hiring out some of your work, you may have an opportunity to rest and recharge. You may find that having just one less demand will help reduce your stress level.

Chapter Four

I AM HUMAN

I Am Enough

When was the last time you felt that who you are and what you do each day is enough? Have you thought about it much? Can you name three people who changed the world for good on a global scale? Can you name ten more? How about one hundred more individuals? That top one-hundred list is a bit more difficult to create. If you didn't name yourself in the top three people who changed the world for good on a global scale, you are in the company of billions of others who didn't either. Does that make the rest of us less than or just on a different path? I never aspired to be a famous surgeon or inventor. But I do love the life I created, and I love being a parent.

Can you name people you positively impact daily, weekly, or monthly? Why is it important to think about the people you care for regularly? At the end of each day, there is a long list of things that didn't get done. This can leave you feeling overwhelmed, frustrated, and feeling like you didn't accomplish enough. If you look at the big picture items, you accomplished something meaningful even if the dirty dishes sit in the sink overnight.

Child care provides:

- Education, such as reading and math skills
- Help reaching developmental milestones
- Relationship skills
- Morals and values
- Health and fitness
- Happiness
- Self-esteem
- And more

Career or work provides:

- Housing
- Food
- Clothing
- Transportation
- Vacations
- And more

Life Goals

Making time to care for yourself may seem like building a ladder to the moon. If you have children at home, teaching them to care for their own needs and interests is important. You need to support and model this behavior. Plus, running on empty and having mommy tantrums doesn't help your children's self-esteem or yours. If you are caring for a senior, carving out time for yourself becomes even more important. You are taking on so many more responsibilities, decisions, and stress being a parent's caregiver.

Which one of these areas below do you think needs the most attention? Why? Can you set aside 15 minutes a day to think about how you want to change that aspect of your life?

- Health
- Career
- Finances
- Relationships
- Spirituality
- Parenting
- Personal growth
- Hobbies and interests
- Meditation
- Other

What is your number one goal? When can you make time each day for this goal? Can you set an alarm or reminder on your phone? By starting small, you can start carving out time for yourself without feeling guilty. Your happiness and mental, emotional, and physical health are vital not only for you but also for the people you love. If you make the goal too big, it will remain on the to-do list. The idea is to start very small to overcome the procrastination hurdle.

I am not paid to promote MindValley.com. However, the courses have worked so well for me that I wanted to share the site here. The methods and ideas certainly are not for everyone. However, it is important to find an app, program, book, group, or other platform to help you work toward your goals.

Recently, I started meditating and attending yoga classes several days a week. I also began creating artwork again and posted a few things on FineArtAmerica.com. The point is that I am creating meaning outside of caring for my family, working, visiting my mother, and doing chores. Fifteen minutes a day will help you establish a routine and habit of self-care without adversely impacting anyone. Your family is likely to notice you becoming happier, healthier, and more like your old self again. Every one of us in the sandwich generation is missing our old selves to some degree. I tear up just thinking about how carefree and simple life was at one time. But I also acknowledge that although it was fun, it wasn't fulfilling.

Chapter Five

SUCCESS AT HOME

Perfectionism & Unrealistic Expectations

S pencer vs the house. Picture a 50-pound mud pit racing through every room, jumping on every piece of furniture in your home. In less than 60 seconds, he can create several hours' worth of work if he escapes my grip at the door. He is a lovable tornado. I often think his life would have been miserable if he had been with another family. Would they keep him? Would he be re-homed over and over? Despite numerous trainers and countless hours of training, he is still a free spirit with a huge zest for life that will not be squelched. Perhaps he is doing something right.

During the mud seasons (winter, spring, and fall in northeast Ohio), clean floors last a few hours if I am lucky. I would need to dedicate hours every day to cleaning up after Spencer. Since he is a six-years-old dog, it is unlikely he is going to change. I had to adjust my expectations. I clean the floors once or twice a week. Usually, we just have dirty floors.

Teen desk. Just walk away. I just need to walk away. Honestly, my desk looks the same way at times. But I can't leave it a mess for long. My teenage son seems to enjoy his nest. He has his own space in the basement. So, I embrace the out-of-sight, out-of-mind principle. It is yet another lesson in picking my battles. I could fight, argue, and push my goals on him or allow him to have his space how he likes it and enjoy a more harmonious relationship. He will soon be off to college, so I choose happiness.

Sandwich Generation Caregivers

When you wake up one day in the sandwich generation, caring for a senior parent as well as your children, your workload instantly doubles. It is more than just more appointments or errands. It can feel like you are now the parent of your parent since you are responsible for his/her home maintenance, meals, medical, legal and financial decisions. You take on an entire second household full of duties and obligations. If that isn't enough, many baby boomer generation individuals have a love affair with their things and each item is of the highest value in their mind. By using the worksheets in this book, you can set expectations and come to an agreement on many decisions. More on that later.

Chapter Six

MORE REASONS TO GET ORGANIZED

Why is Organizing Your Home So Important?

Wasteful spending and lost production time can kill a business. Yet, many of us do not take into consideration that wasteful spending and lost production at home negatively impact our health, happiness, free time, relationships, and finances. If you are overrun with household chores, you have little time for yourself, your family, or healthy habits.

Today, our homes are bursting at the seams with a wide assortment of items. For instance, many of our homes have products or tools for the following businesses and professions:

- Landscaper
- Interior decorator
- Painter

- Home improvement contractor
- Nurse
- Home office
- Teacher
- Chef
- Barber
- Car mechanic
- Laundry mat
- Housekeeping
- Seamstress

Is it any surprise that keeping track of all of these items takes up considerable time and space?

Lastly, shopping is rewarding. Marketing campaigns are designed to convince consumers that a product will instantly and forever improve their lives. In reality, all of us have closets full of broken promises that we will instantly be transformed into flawless, confident, happy, and wealthy individuals. Many product marketing campaigns over-promise and under-deliver.

Think about the big picture. Why do you want to get organized? Do you want to spend less time doing chores? Do you need to reduce monthly spending? Like all chores, organization is a process that is never finished. However, you can make your time more efficient. Begin by writing your organization goal down and hang it on the refrigerator. This will keep it in front of you. Have you thought about making good use of your time while you are waiting for water to boil? You can surf the internet or organize one kitchen drawer in 10 minutes. If you organize one small space a day, in a week your kitchen will be much neater.

Declutter Your Thinking

Setting limits and lifestyle priorities is an important part of getting organized. When you think about possessions as useful items, part of an inventory collection, it is easier to set limits on how many items you use, need, and even want. Maintaining a huge collection of shoes while only routinely wearing five pairs takes time, money, and space.

Establish a new method of maintaining your household inventory. A business must routinely look at its supplies. Make shopping lists. Add products with the quantity needed as you see your stock getting low. Try to stick to the list and not buy on impulse.

When you look back years from now, the time you spent with your family and friends will be memorable. Clean floors, toys, gadgets, and personal items will be easily forgotten. Simplify and reduce your personal and household inventory to make quality time.

Declutter Your Home

Declutter low-value items before you organize. The goal here is to reduce unnecessary items. This frees up space, reduces the number of items you need to sort and organize, and reduces your overall inventory. Gather like with like so you can see your entire inventory. For instance, gather all your magazines to evaluate the entire collection. Will you read them again? How long have you had them? Be sure to check off each task as you finish it. This will give you a sense of accomplishment, especially as the to-do list shrinks and the completed list grows.

Recycle, shred, donate, or throw away these items.

- Old newspapers
- Old magazines
- Old books

- Old files (shred)
- Old office supplies
- Old cleaning supplies such as rags or mops
- Old or damaged home goods
- Old or damaged home decor
- Old or damaged toys
- Old or damaged furniture
- Damaged clothing
- Expired food and spices

Now that you have removed some of the excess, evaluating the remaining items is less taxing. When you have fewer items, you have less decisions to make. For each remaining item, you can consider whether or not the item is needed or wanted and where it is best to store it. While it may seem overwhelming to consider EVERY item in your home, some items are quite easy. For instance, you can make decisions about your current furniture very quickly. Most of your furniture is in use or storage. Items in use are likely items you want to keep. Therefore, when you are looking at bedroom organization, it comes down to just evaluating and organizing clothing, shoes and accessories.

The individual steps to easily organize your home are provided in Chapter 8. Whole home decluttering is addressed in greater detail in Step 2. You will also have the opportunity to address unused items in each room. The reason this is repeated is to create space for the items you enjoy by removing the items you do not use, want, or need. Too often, we will go out a buy a few new articles of clothing, increasing the number of items in our closet without removing the old, worn-out items we no longer use. You might be surprised just how many unused household and personal items you are currently storing in your home.

Chapter Seven

SETTING PRIORITIES

Home Organization Questionnaire

Filing out a simple questionnaire doesn't take long, but it is time well spent. After you evaluate how each area of your home is functioning, you can establish a simple plan and goal for each area. The way this worksheet is structured may seem very redundant. However, it allows you to walk from one room into the next and address the questions specific to that area.

Kitchen, food cupboards or pantry

- Easy to find things
- Easy to clean and keep clean
- Cluttered, too much stuff
- Cluttered, disorganized
- Solution: better storage
- Solution: better organization

Kitchen, storage cupboards & drawers

- Easy to find things
- Easy to clean and keep clean
- Cluttered, too much stuff
- Cluttered, disorganized
- Solution: better storage
- Solution: better organization

Kitchen, utensils areas

- Easy to find things
- Easy to clean and keep clean
- Cluttered, too much stuff
- Cluttered, disorganized
- Solution: better storage
- Solution: better organization

Kitchen, small appliances

- Easy to find things
- Easy to clean and keep clean
- Cluttered, too much stuff
- Cluttered, disorganized
- Solution: better storage
- Solution: better organization

Laundry/Mud Room cupboards, shelves, drawers

- Easy to find things
- Easy to clean and keep clean

- Cluttered, too much stuff
- Cluttered, disorganized
- Solution: better storage
- Solution: better organization

Laundry soaps & cleaning supplies

- Easy to find things
- Easy to clean and keep clean
- Cluttered, too much stuff
- Cluttered, disorganized
- Solution: better storage
- Solution: better organization

Laundry area

- Sorted & ready to be washed
- Collapsible laundry basket
- Place to hang clean clothes
- Cluttered, disorganized
- Solution: better storage
- Solution: better organization

Family/Living Room

- Easy to find things
- Easy to clean and keep clean
- Cluttered, too much stuff
- Cluttered, disorganized
- Solution: better storage
- Solution: better organization

Dining Room

- Easy to find things
- Easy to clean and keep clean
- Cluttered, too much stuff
- Cluttered, disorganized
- Solution: better storage
- Solution: better organization

Office/Study

- Easy to find things
- Easy to clean and keep clean
- Cluttered, too much stuff
- Cluttered, disorganized
- Solution: better storage
- Solution: better organization

Bedrooms

- Easy to find things
- Easy to clean and keep clean
- Cluttered, too much stuff
- Cluttered, disorganized
- Solution: better storage
- Solution: better organization

Closets

- Easy to find things
- Easy to clean and keep clean
- Cluttered, too much stuff

- Cluttered, disorganized
- Solution: better storage
- Solution: better organization

Basement/Storage

- Easy to find things
- Easy to clean and keep clean
- Cluttered, too much stuff
- Cluttered, disorganized
- Solution: better storage
- Solution: better organization

Garage

- Easy to find things
- Easy to clean and keep clean
- Cluttered, too much stuff
- Cluttered, disorganized
- Solution: better storage
- Solution: better organization

Summary and Plan for Your Rooms

Now, set your priorities. Choose an area to start then find the corresponding worksheet for that area in the Table of Contents. If you prefer to have a printed worksheet, you will find the Essential Home Organization LLC website and access code in the Introduction section of this book. You can download and print all of the worksheets at no additional cost. If your family is working with you, it might be helpful if you can cross off the listed tasks as you complete them. Consider offering a reward like going to the park when you are finished.

If you decide to start in the kitchen, jump to the Kitchen Worksheet. If you determine you have too many items, focus on the goal of reducing your inventory. You may want to write out the goal on a sheet of paper to help you stay focused on the solution. Use the Kitchen Worksheet to organize your items. Can you move mail sorting to another room? Can homework be done elsewhere? Can you reduce the number of small kitchen appliances? After you toss out expired food, do you have enough space? Are you using all of the utensils? There are many ways to reduce inventory in a room, especially the kitchen.

Chapter Eight

EASY ORGANIZATION

Step 1: Prepare Sorting Labels

You can create Sorting Labels yourself with 3x5 notecards or any paper you have on hand. Color coding is very helpful. You can use colored paper or colored markers.

Grouping all donations by pink label makes things fast and easy to gather and remove from your home. More importantly, it helps separate the items you want to keep from the items you plan to sell or throw away. Include the date and contents on each card if you are putting items into storage. This will save you tremendous time and frustration when you need to find stored items.

Create separate labels for each category.

- Keep
- Undecided
- Sell

- Donate
- Recycle
- Trash

Step 2: Declutter

Unnecessary household inventory is also known as clutter. Go on a trash, donation, and recycling collecting mission. If you have already made up your mind to get rid of specific items, this will reduce your workload by reducing your inventory. Look for items you can easily part with today. Take the time to get rid of those items to open up space. This is the best place to start any organization project.

Organizing is about progress, not perfection. Start by eliminating excess and unused items in each category before you try to organize or set up finished rooms. Once that's done, put items together in labeled bins, on shelves, or in dedicated closets. You can then sort and eliminate more items. With everything in its place, you can easily move items around as you determine room uses.

Minimalism might be trendy, but most of us enjoy our stuff. Where many of us fail is that we don't part with things that no longer serve a purpose. If you haven't worn a T-shirt for two years, it doesn't serve a purpose for you. But, it can serve a purpose for someone else.

These items are fairly easy to declutter. Start with the easiest items first to enjoy immediate results.

Family heirlooms

- Broken furniture in the basement, garage, or attic
- Old photographs that sit in a box

- Can you photograph any items?
- Check with family members before parting with family treasures.
- Antiques may have a high value. Look for things that are broken and worn for now.

Cleaning supplies

- Old cleaners
- Cleaners that didn't work well
- Old mops, brushes, vacuums
- Old rags
- Excess buckets, brushes, etc.

Entertainment

- Books
- CDs
- DVDs
- Magazine subscriptions - digital or print
- Photographs

Holiday decorations

- Items you no longer use
- Old, worn out, or outgrown items

Home decor

- Items not in use
- Consider relocating or refurbishing

Pet supplies

- Items no longer in use
- Old, damaged toys
- Items that didn't work well for your pet

School projects and supplies

- Photograph special items
- Donate/sell musical equipment
- Donate/sell textbooks
- Create a scrapbook or photo book

Tools

- Old or broken power tools
- Old or broken hand tools
- Old paint supplies

Yard and Gardening

- Broken shovels, rakes etc.
- Unused hand tools
- Excess or broken planters

Toys

Sorting toys can get a little complicated because there are so many different types of items and age ranges. But sorting by category first and then by condition will make the job much simpler because you can evaluate one small group at a time. After they are grouped, you can easily store like with like, which makes it easier for your children to find their favorite items and put them away.

Step 1: Gather and Sort by Category

- Action figures
- Books
- Cars, trucks etc.
- Dolls
- Stuffed animals
- Electronics

Step 2: Sort by Condition

- New (keep)
- Favorite or special (keep)
- Outgrown (donate, sell, trash)
- Missing parts or broken (trash)

Step 3: Select a Method for the Day

After you have decluttered and you are ready to begin organizing, choose a method. How do you want to approach the day? Do you want to tackle a big project or tidy up one or two kitchen drawers? Try different methods and see which one works best for you.

Go big: Choose a room that will give you a big impact fast, such as the garage. Be prepared for all the detail work. Be sure to label incomplete bins and boxes as **Undecided** so you know where you left off last time. Anytime you tackle a large project, the detailed work may need to be finished later.

Easy does it: Choose a simple project to complete. Mark it off your checklist when finished. This will give you more checkmarks on your checklist faster and easier. This may be the way to go if you are suffering from low motivation or feeling overwhelmed. Perhaps you just want to sort books today.

Get it together: Go on a mission to put like with like. Gather items and place them in a designated area to be sorted later.

Step 4: Gather

Do you remember how fun treasure hunts were when you were a kid? If you have small children, you can turn their help into a game. Select an item, such as books, and see how many they can bring to you.

Step 5: Sort

1. Prepare. Make sorting labels and tape them onto bins or boxes. Create the following labels: **Keep**, **Undecided**, **Donate**, **Sell**, **Recycle**, **Trash**. The following steps will keep your work organized, making sorting easier.

2. Gather like with like. Focus on one grouping at a time. For instance, lay out all of your black dress shoes. Do you wear all of them? Has it been a while?

3. Put your favorite items back into the closet or into a storage bin labeled **Keep**. Date and write the contents on the label. When you want to find items later, this will save you considerable time.

4. Remove the items you no longer want or use. Put them in the **Trash**, **Donate**, or **Sell** bins. After this step, you should see the results of your effort!

5. Address the remaining items. Sorting can be very tedious. Take breaks. Come back to sorting when you are fresher. If you have had enough, put items in a box or bin labeled **Undecided** and sort the items later.

Step 6: Dealing with Indecision

You have made great progress! You chose your favorite items, put them where they will used, or stored them in a bin labeled **Keep.** You are already making decisions. The first task is to simply acknowledge that you are making progress and to stay positive! Staying motivated, especially when you are just starting out, is its own task.

Now, you are faced with the **Undecided** group of items, which are the most difficult to sort. You likely have mixed thoughts or feelings about this group. This group of items takes the longest to sort because it is not clear what you should do with them. The following questions may help you make decisions about **Undecided** items: Do I use this item? How often? Do I have similar items I use more often? Do I still want, need, or enjoy it? Is this an "I might use it someday" item? Did I buy it on sale? Do I really like it, or was it a bargain?

Lastly, wait it out. Store things and come back to them later. Include the date and contents on the label then place the bin in storage. If a year goes by and you don't miss the items, chances are you don't really want or need them.

Step 7: Focus on Function

Your household items need to be perfectly placed, NOT perfectly put away. Focus on function first rather than the appearance of your storage system. Beautiful baskets may look amazing, but what do you do if they do not hold enough items? Try to place items where they are used first then make decisions about storage. If possible, try to get through as many of your household items first before you go out and buy storage bins or baskets. You may already have items you can use. In addition, you may decide that room uses are not working well together. If you decide to move the video game console to the basement, you open up space in the family room for other items.

Consider your storage carefully. I tried the cute little labeled jar concept for my kitchen and quickly abandoned it. It takes time to maintain, and I didn't find it helpful. Instead of having one jar of rice, I had a jar of rice that was almost gone and a box of rice waiting for the jar to become empty. I don't want to mix old and new food items. Of course, I also felt the need to wash the jar once it was empty. Then, I had to wait for it to be completely dry.... My engineering mind went crazy over all of the "necessary" tasks to store rice. What a waste of time and energy! Yes, I can and do laugh at myself.

Step 8: Reflect on Time

You are likely thinking, "I don't have time for all of this!" That is absolutely true, in a way. But you also don't have time to waste. You will save time and energy if everyone knows where things belong! Keep the big picture in mind while you are working. Your home has limited space. Why store things that have little or no value? If it isn't being used, it is clutter. Maintaining clutter creates more work, less space, more disorganization and provides little to no benefit. Remember, for every area of your home that stays neat and organized, you save time and energy every week. A dirty home takes time to clean. A dirty and disorganized home takes far more time and energy to clean every week.

Do The Math!

If you save just 1 hour every week, you save 52 hours over the course of a year. If you save 2 hours a week, you save 104 hours. Consider that 104 hours is equal to 13 eight-hour workdays! What could you do for yourself with those extra hours?

Chapter Nine

DO THINGS YOUR WAY

___

Jump Ahead!

While we all have many of the same items in our homes, our approach to cleaning and organizing is unique. Each worksheet lays out the tasks and provides simple instructions to gather, sort, and store. However, how you approach each step and when you do one room or another is completely up to you. When my kitchen needs attention, sometimes I tackle one drawer. Sometimes, I spend an afternoon pulling out every item from the cupboards and drawers to clean and re-organize.

It's just fifteen minutes. You can use it or waste it every day. Plus, it adds up. If you used 15 minutes a day productively for 365 days, you would have over 90 hours of time you put to good use throughout the year. That is equal to eleven 8-hour work days! In 15 minutes, you can shred papers. You can create sorting labels for your next organization project. You can organize one drawer. You can sort a stack of papers. You can deliberately sit down, close your eyes, breath, and rest. Or you can watch dog or cat videos. There is nothing wrong with being unproductive if you are choosing to rest and recharge. However, you can also start a load of laundry before starting dinner to tackle two things at once. How can you be more effective without exhausting yourself? I try to get as much done in the kitchen as I can while I wait for dinner to cook. I routinely wash dishes as I prepare dinner to have fewer dishes after we eat. I don't enjoy cooking or doing dishes, so I try to be as efficient as possible.

I organized this book to provide easy access to any worksheet by checking the Table of Contents. Each worksheet was designed to give you the necessary information without the burden of excessive reading. I specifically designed the worksheets to be effective, and they are most definitely not works of art. The worksheets are guides to help you increase the organization of your home, help interior spaces function more smoothly, and reduce your workload.

Chapter 10 includes home organization worksheets for all areas of your home. Chapters 11 and 12 provide worksheets to tackle downsizing and moving. These topics are included because moving is going to be necessary at some point.

Chapter Ten

HOME ORGANIZATION WORKSHEETS

Donation Plan

Make space for the things that you use and enjoy by removing unwanted and unnecessary items. Choose a drop-off location or schedule a pick-up for your donations. Be sure to write down the donation center's address, hours, and phone number.

Consider donating these items:

- Clothes and shoes
- Furniture and decor
- Home goods
- Blankets and bedding
- Office supplies
- Books

- CDs,
- DVDs
- Toys

Locations that may accept donations include:

- Thrift stores
- Homeless shelters
- Women's shelters
- Veteran's charities
- Libraries may take books, CDs and DVDs
- Churches
- The Salvation Army
- Google "donate stuff near me" for more ideas

Recycling may be available at:

- Churches
- Schools
- City municipal buildings
- Fire departments
- Police departments

Also consider:

- eBay, Craigslist, Nextdoor, etc.
- Junk hauling companies
- Bagster for remodeling debris
- Garage sales
- Pet shelters may take cleaning supplies, pet supplies, used towels

Kitchen Organization

Form Follows Function

What does that mean? Simply put, your kitchen's function is the first thing to consider rather than its appearance. Designer pantry jars may not function well in your home if you are an avid chef. Remember, most of your guests will not see inside your pantry, so select items that perform well.

Before You Start

Since you prepare and eat in your kitchen daily, prioritize storing items you need to prepare meals in the most convenient spaces. Frequently used items should be easy to find, easy to use, and easy to put away. After all, how long does it take before the kitchen floor gets dirty and the sink is overflowing with dirty dishes? Life is fast and messy so cleaning I up should be fast and easy. If you use the kitchen work space for homework, crafts, and mail sorting, it might be best to store related items in a different location if you have limited space in the kitchen.

1. Consider time management. Organizing your kitchen will be a messy process. Allow plenty of time to pull things out of cupboards, clean the cupboard, and return items. You can do just one cupboard or one drawer at a time and complete the kitchen over a week.

2. Design your new layout before you begin. Create the labels below for your items and tape them to each cupboard, drawer, and storage area. Laying out your kitchen before moving items around keeps things tidy. Plus you can stop in the middle of the project and pick it back up later. Keep your labels in place for a while until you get used to the new storage system. Just be sure the tape or other adhesive does not damage the surfaces.

- Baking mixes
- Baking dishes
- Beverages
- Blender
- Bowls
- Coffee & tea
- Cookie sheets
- Cooling racks
- Cups & mugs
- Electric skillet
- Flour
- Lids
- Measuring cups
- Measuring spoons
- Medications
- Mixer
- Mixing bowls
- Noodles
- Oils
- Oven mitts
- Pans
- Plates
- Popcorn maker
- Pots
- Pressure cooker
- Rice
- Rice cooker
- Spices
- Strainers
- Storage
- Sugar
- Towels
- Utensils
- Vinegar
- Vitamins
- Waffle maker
- Wok

3. Consider where you want to place things. Put things you rarely use in hard-to-reach places and things you use daily close at hand.
4. Remove items from one storage area at a time.
5. Sort and group like with like. Store canned soups together. Store noodles and rice together.
6. Remove expired items and place them in the trash.
7. Begin the next area, grouping like with like and removing out-of- date items.
8. Return items to cupboards following your newly designed layout. Try to put the items that will expire soon in the front.

9. For non-food items, use sorting labels to make different piles for **Keep, Donate, Recycle, and Trash.** You can make these labels on 3x5 note cards or any paper you have available. Gather like with like. Then, evaluate each grouping. You may not realize you have five spatulas you never use. Every item takes up space. Even the small items create unnecessary clutter, making it more difficult to find the things you want and need.

Kitchen Storage

Prepared food storage containers are often a hassle with missing lids or missing bottoms. Try Bentgo or other containers. Bentgo food prep containers are affordable and lightweight. They are easy to clean, stack, and store. I love them so much that I have given Bentgo containers as gifts! They can be used to store other items such as batteries, pens, and craft supplies as well.

Cabinets will stay neater if you invest in clear plastic bins with open tops. They allow you to group and store small items such as vitamins or tea boxes neatly. The bins also maximize the use of higher shelving since it is easy to pull the bin out and return it after use. Clear plastic bins also keep your refrigerator neater.

Designer pantries may not work for you. Think about storage containers that will work the best for you, not look the best. For example, what do you do when you run low on flour? Do you add the new flour on top or store the new box of flour in the cupboard until you empty the pretty storage container? Be sure your storage solutions save either time or space, depending on your goal.

Bedroom Organization

Keeping clothing and accessories neat and orderly can be frustrating. We have items for many occasions and seasons. In fact, it is possible to have a wide selection of T-shirts, with some for yard work, others for exercise, and still others for an evening out. When you begin sorting, take the time to gather very similar things and evaluate them as one group. Put away your favorites and then look at the items that remain. Are any of them worn and old? Remove those items next. Lastly, look at the remaining items. Do they fit well? Do you wear everything regularly?

Use the Sorting Labels - **Keep**, **Undecided**, **Sell**, **Donate**, and **Trash** - to create separate piles. Place a checkmark next to each category when finished. Parting with just a few items from each group will add up and provide more space for the items you enjoy.

Clothing

- Work shirts
- Work pants
- Dresses
- Skirts
- Jeans
- Shirts/tops
- Blazers
- Sweaters
- Undergarments
- Socks
- Shorts
- Sleeveless shirts/tops
- Swimwear

Footwear

- Work shoes
- Dress shoes

- High heels
- Sandals
- Hiking boots
- Work boots
- Athletic shoes

Personal Care

- Make-up
- Skincare
- Hair care
- Nail care
- Soaps
- Lotions
- Perfume
- Cologne

Accessories

- Jewelry
- Scarves
- Ties
- Belts
- Handbags
- Wallets

Outerwear

- Lightweight coats
- Winter coats

- Winter boots
- Work boots
- Hats
- Scarves
- Gloves

Garage Organization

Whether you're a DIY enthusiast or just someone who loves to garden, there's no garage that's immune to a little disorder. With a little creativity, you can transform chaos into order and create the perfect space for all your items.

Step 1: Gather and Sort by Category

- Lawn and garden items
- Sports equipment
- Tools
- Bikes/toys
- Car care

Step 2: Sort and Store

- Lawn and garden
  - Remove old, unused and broken items.
  - Dispose of unwanted fertilizers and chemicals.
  - Hang rakes, shovels, and trimmers on a wall.
- Sports equipment
  - Donate or sell unused items.
  - Discard old, worn, and broken items.
  - Buy designated sports storage solutions such as golf bag racks and heavy-duty bins for equipment.

- Hardware and tools
  - Use old jars or designated plastic containers.
  - Separate by type and size.
  - Buy a specialty hanging system for hand tools.
  - Buy a tool chest.
  - Discard old, worn, broken items.
  - Donate or sell unused items.
- Toys and bikes
  - Buy designated storage solutions.
  - Wall-mounted bike racks save floor space.
  - Remove old, worn, and broken items.
  - Sell or donate unused items.
- Car care
  - Remove unwanted items.
  - Group like with like.
    - Washes
    - Polishes
    - Fluids
    - Parts

Step 3: Buy Storage Solutions

Before you choose any storage, evaluate the space you have available. Can you move items around in the garage to open up more space? Can you use shelves that are attached to the ceiling to open up more floor space? Consider wall racks and mounts, too. Do some homework on Wayfair, Lowes, and Home Depot. You might find new ideas.

Keep in mind if you need permanent storage or temporary storage. There are plenty of heavy-duty plastic shelving options that can be put together quickly without tools and stored easily when not in use. I have several heavy-duty plastic shelving units and find them the most versatile, affordable, and lightweight.

Basement & Storage

The variety of items people store is vast. Many items on the included checklist may not apply to your situation. To begin, cross out the items you do not have so you can focus on the items you need to sort. Then, start with the fastest and largest items to sort. Your goal is to reduce your unused household inventory with the least amount of effort. This will help you feel like you are making great progress. What specific goal do you want to accomplish today? Two hours of focused attention is better than spending hours feeling overwhelmed. Try to avoid pulling everything into the middle of the room unless your goal is simply to group like with like to store and then sort later.

If you are procrastinating because the job is large, you can also start with easy things such as old newspapers, magazines, and expired food. You can also choose to just start with something fast and simple such as cleaning supplies. When you have a narrow focus, you are able to achieve your task. When you look at the entire project as one big job, you are likely to walk away and enjoy your favorite snack. Who hasn't looked at a task and put it off? Keep in mind that you are reducing clutter to make room for the items you use and enjoy and that this is a process.

You have seen this same list before. It is very common to store things you use regularly in the main living area of your home and store similar items in the basement or storage areas. Remember to have your sorting labels ready. Consider having boxes or bins labeled before you begin to make it easy to toss things into the appropriate container. This will eliminate confusion and reduce frustration.

Cleaning supplies

- Old cleaners
- Cleaners that didn't work well
- Old mops, brushes, vacuums
- Old rags
- Excess buckets, brushes, etc.

Entertainment

- Books
- CDs
- DVDs
- Magazine subscriptions - digital or print
- Photographs

Family heirlooms

- Broken furniture in the basement, garage, or attic
- Old photographs that sit in a box
- Can you photograph any items?
- Check with family members before parting with family treasures.
- Antiques may have a high value. Look for things that are broken and worn for now.

Holiday decorations

- Old, worn out, outgrown
- Items you no longer use

Home decor

- Items not in use
- Consider relocating or refurbishing

Pet supplies

- Items not in use
- Old or broken toys
- Items that didn't work well for your pet

School projects and supplies

- Photograph special items
- Donate/sell musical equipment
- Donate/sell textbooks
- Create a scrapbook or photo book

Tools

- Old or broken power tools
- Old or broken hand tools
- Old paint supplies

Yard and gardening

- Broken shovels, rakes etc.
- Unused hand tools
- Excess or broken planters

Toys

Toys get a little complicated because there are so many different types of items and age ranges. But sorting by category first and then by condition will make the job much simpler because you can evaluate one small group at a time. After they are grouped, you can easily store like with like, which makes it easier for your children to find their favorite items and put them away.

Gather and Sort by Category

- Action figures
- Books
- Cars, trucks etc.
- Dolls
- Stuffed animals
- Electronics

Sort by Condition

- New (keep)
- Favorite or special (keep)
- Outgrown (donate, sell, trash)
- Missing parts or broken (trash)

Storage solutions

Before you choose any storage, evaluate the space you have available, measuring length, width, and height. You can check Wayfair, Lowes, and Home Depot for ideas. However, I have several heavy-duty plastic shelving units and find them the most versatile, affordable, and lightweight. They are also great to use in damp conditions.

The fabric square collapsible bins are fantastic for toy storage. They are inexpensive and lightweight. Children will not get injured using them. They are easy to store when not in use. Lastly, children will outgrow their toys and the need for storage.

Helpful Hint: You have seen the same instructions — declutter, create sorting labels, gather, and sort — a number of times. You are developing a new set of skills and a method that will become an easy routine. Do you think about doing laundry, or do you just do it? Home organization is no different. It is just a skill. Repetition helps us learn skills and create new habits.

Important Papers

Your important records will be easy to find with an organized filing system. Choose the method that works best for you. How do you look for things? Do you search by company name like Lowes or by subject like Home Improvement? A DYMO label maker will help make labeling files quick and easy. Decide if new documents are in the front or the back of each file.

Method A: Sort files by category, then alphabetically. Use different colored folders.

Examples:

- Use blue file folders for everything relating to your automobiles, such as financing, insurance, maintenance, and title.

- Use orange file folders for your home, including appliances, insurance, mortgage and repairs. You can use one orange file or create separate files for each group. You would have one for appliances, one for insurance, one for mortgage, and so forth.

- Use green file folders for your pet. Create a green file for licenses, vet bills, and vet records. You can put everything pet in one green folder or create a unique green file folder for vets bills, another for licenses, and another for vet records.

Method B: Sort files by company. This is the simplest method and the one I prefer. You can use just one folder color for all files. Create a separate file folder for each company and file in alphabetical order.

- Bank of America
- Chase
- Home Depot
- Lowes

Method C: Sort files by subject first and then by company. You can use different colored folders or keep things uniform. You can create labels in this format.

- Credit: Bank of America
- Credit: Chase
- Phone: Verizon
- Insurance: Aetna
- Insurance: State Farm

Sorting Papers

Step 1: Create sorting labels for your stacks of paper to pre-sort. You can simply use markers and write on copy paper. Make separate labels for **To-do**, **File**, **Shred**, and **Trash.** Spread the labeled papers out on your work surface. Do not worry about creating order in each stack. Just sort first. **To-do** is for bills that need to be paid or other work that needs your attention.

Step 2: Shed papers and take out the trash. These two tasks are fairly quick and give you great visual results.

Step 3: Tackle filing. Begin by making stacks. Grouping by company name is the easiest way to sort. Once you have some stacks made, you can begin creating file folder labels. Place the items in the file. You can organize the papers in each file after your stack of papers is sorted and in individual files. This is an ongoing process. However, you can use this same method to organize future stacks of papers.

Step 4: Electronic documents. Create a log-in list on your computer. Include the company name, your username, and password. It is best to write your passwords in pencil since they often change. This also prevents hackers from accessing them. Store this document in a safe place.

Step 5: Start working on your **To-do** stack. Then, file, shred, or throw away papers when finished.

Step 6: Daily Maintenance. Place a **To-do** and a **Shred** file in your kitchen or on your entry table. This will allow you to sort incoming mail daily. Recycle junk mail daily.

Digital Photographs

Most of us have digital photos stored on more than one device. This is a complex category that can be time-consuming to organize. However, once you create a written outline, it will be easy to create electronic folders in the same format. Once organized, you will be able to easily enjoy your photos on a device, order prints, and create photo books.

Method A: Sort by date, then by topic. Create photo folders for each topic.

- 2015 Family Photos (year)
  - 2015 Disney Trip
  - 2015 Beach Trip
  - 2015 Sledding
- 2016 Family Photos (year)
  - 2016 Andrew's Birthday Party
  - 2016 Thanksgiving

Method B: Sort by subject, then by date. Create photo folders for each topic.

- Chris and Bobby (subject)
  - 2015 Sledding
  - 2015 Beach Trip
- Bailey (subject)
  - 2015 Puppy pictures
  - 2016 Obedience class

Method C: Sort by subject only. All photos, regardless of date, go into one folder. For example, you can put all of your dog Bailey's photos in one folder.

Method D: Sort by date only. All photos from one calendar year, regardless of subject, go into one folder. You could choose to use either Method C or Method D, to begin with and then create subfolders later.

Steps to Organize Your Photos:

1. BACK UP YOUR FILES! Use an external hard drive or keep a backup online.

2. Create an outline on paper. Then, use the outline to create electronic folders in the same format.

3. Move digital images into their designated folders. You can move all 2015 Trips into one folder first and then create folders for individual trips.

4. BACK UP AGAIN! Label the folder "Revised Photo Folders" or other names to indicate the photos are organized.

5. Consider making physical copies of your favorite photos to enjoy each day.

Expense Tracking

Tracking your finances is one of the most important things you can do to prevent financial hardships. Use the information below to create a monthly worksheet in a Word or Excel document. By tracking and analyzing each month, you can determine if you need to make changes to accomplish your goals.

All worksheets are available with your book purchase at www. essentialhomeorganization.com if you prefer to download and print them. See the Introduction section of this book for more details.

Summary for: (month/year)

- Total income: $ _____
- Total savings: $ _____
- Total expenses: $ _____
- Total: $ _____

Housing Costs: $_____

- Mortgage/rent
- Home equity loan
- Heating/cooling
- Electric
- TV
- Internet
- Water
- Sewer
- Lawn care
- Cleaning service
- Security
- Repairs
- Misc

Transportation: $ _____

- Car loan
- Fuel
- Maintenance
- Parking
- Public transportation

Insurance: $ _____

- Home/Renter
- Auto
- Health

- Dental
- Vision
- Misc.
- Misc.

Food: $ _____

- Groceries
- Dining out
- Beverages

Education: $ _____

- Tuition
- Tuition
- Loans
- Loans

Personal Care: $ _____

- Clothing
- Shoes
- Accessories
- Hair cuts
- Manicures
- Misc.
- Misc.
- Misc.

Health: $ _____

- Gym
- Prescriptions
- Supplements
- Vision self-pay
- Dental self-pay

Childcare: $ _____

- Daycare
- Nanny
- Babysitter
- School expenses

Pets: $ _____

- Licenses
- Vet bills
- Daycare
- Boarding
- Dog walker

Credit Cards: $ _____

Misc: $ _____

Health and Wellness

Prepare and Achieve Goals

1. **Prepare:** Print this plan and hang it on the refrigerator to help you make better nutritional choices.

2. **Set a Health Goal:** "I am committed to having more strength and energy."

3. **Make a Plan:** Write down an activity for each day of the week. Add your time, distance, or other goal.

4. **Execute:** Check off the box after completing the activity each day.

5. **Adjust:** Change your plans to increase your duration or activity. Changing your exercise routine will also help to keep it fresh and provide greater challenge.

6. **Use Tools:** Apps may be useful if you already rely on them. However, having the Health and Exercise Worksheet on the refrigerator can help you stay on track. It is very easy to dismiss electronic reminders.

7. **Focus on Mindset:** Focus on wellness, health, increased stamina, increased strength, or your favorite outfit rather than a long list of things you think you should avoid. It is a daily lifestyle choice to prioritize mental, emotional, and physical well-being.

8. **Measure:** Create a worksheet and keep completed documents in a folder or 3-ring binder to track your progress. You will achieve large goals by completing smaller daily tasks.

9. **Create a Health Plan with positive goals.** A positive goal can be having two cups of coffee instead of three. A positive goal moves you in the right direction. The word diet makes me think about cookies and cake. Instead, I try to focus on the healthy goals I want to accomplish.

Health Goal:

Exercise Goal:

Date:

Food and Beverage Plan

- Daily ounces of water
- Servings of fresh fruit
- Servings of fresh vegetables
- Servings of caffeine
- Servings of sugar
- Servings of fast food
- Servings of pop/soda
- Servings of chips/refined foods

Daily Exercise Plan

- Walk (distance or time)
- Jog (distance or time)
- Yoga
- Lift weights

Medications and Vitamins

A written Medication and Vitamin Plan will help you stay on schedule. It will also make filling a pill sorter faster and easier if you use one. More importantly, a written schedule in your cabinet will help medical personnel if you have a medical emergency.

Since every individual's needs vary, it may be helpful to create a document on your computer that you can print weekly.

Also, consider using 3x5 notecards to help you keep track of what you need to take next. For example, create a card for each time of day and list the medications or supplements that should be taken at that time. When you take your 6:00 am dose, put that card away and leave the 12:00 pm card out by the kitchen sink. When you take the 12:00 pm doses, put that card away and leave the 5:00 pm dose by the kitchen sink. Be sure to date each card. You may need to revise your cards, and this will eliminate confusion.

3x5 Cards

1. Daily 6:00 am medications and supplements
2. Daily 12:00 pm medications and supplements
3. Daily 5:00 pm medications and supplements
4. Daily 9:00 pm medications and supplements

Routine Chores

While many of us have similar routine chores, they do vary to some degree. A single individual living in Manhattan has a different routine than that of a family of five living on a farm. Feel free to copy and paste this page to create your own chores list. Include a place to assign chores by placing an initial next to the line item. Like all other worksheets, this one is available for download and is included with your book purchase.

Kitchen

- Shop for food
- Clean countertops
- Clean floors
- Clean refrigerator

Bathrooms

- Clean mirrors
- Clean countertops
- Clean toilets
- Clean floors

Laundry Room

- Wash & dry clothes
- Put clothes away
- Clean countertops
- Clean floor

Family Room

- Straighten room
- Clean floor
- Dust

Office

- File & shred papers
- Straighten room
- Clean floor
- Dust

Bedrooms

Straighten room

Clean floor

Dust

Yard Work

- Trim shrubs
- Edge pavement
- Weed wack
- Pick up debris
- Cut grass
- Snow removal

Misc.

- Wash windows
- Clean basement

Room Planning

If you need to make some changes around your home, this worksheet will guide you through the process of creating a more efficient living space. First, focus on each room's use or function. Having incompatible activities in the same room, such as schoolwork and video games, is fuel for ongoing battles.

Begin by making a list of activities for each room and items used for those activities. You can move furniture and items around on a scale drawing before doing any heavy lifting. This way, you can save time and effort and change your mind several times, all while sipping coffee. Once you move furniture into its new location, you can add items that are used in each room. Then, you can consider your storage needs for those items.

Moving isn't easy. Most of us move in, place things were it is convenient at the time, and then struggle with inadequate storage and lost items. When you really consider how each room functions, you can place items where they will be used.

Focus on perfectly placing your household inventory. Items should be easy to find, easy to use, and easy to put away. This single idea will keep your home clutter-free by making it fast and convenient to routinely straighten up rooms.

Create this list for each room. Make sure room activities are compatible to reduce family conflicts.

- Room name
- Activities
- Items for each activity
- Atmosphere: Busy, loud or calm, quiet

Make a Scale Drawing

Making a scale drawing is fairly easy with graph paper. You can find graph paper at office supply stores and many large retailers.

Step 1: Measure your room and write down the dimensions in feet, round to the nearest foot or half foot.

Step 2: Use graph paper and equate one box to one foot. For instance, 10 feet equals 10 boxes. Use a ruler to keep your lines neat.

Step 3: Add openings such as windows and doors. Start at one corner of the room, measure how many feet to the opening, and then measure the width of the opening. Label the opening type, such as a closet door or window.

Step 4: On a second sheet of graph paper, draw simple rectangular shapes to scale for all of your furniture and label them. Using colored pencils might be helpful as well.

Step 5: After you have arranged things, use your cellphone to capture the image and print it. Printed images do not need to be to scale, nor do they need to look perfect. Wouldn't it be nice to hand the room layouts to your movers so your furniture is placed in its best location on moving day?

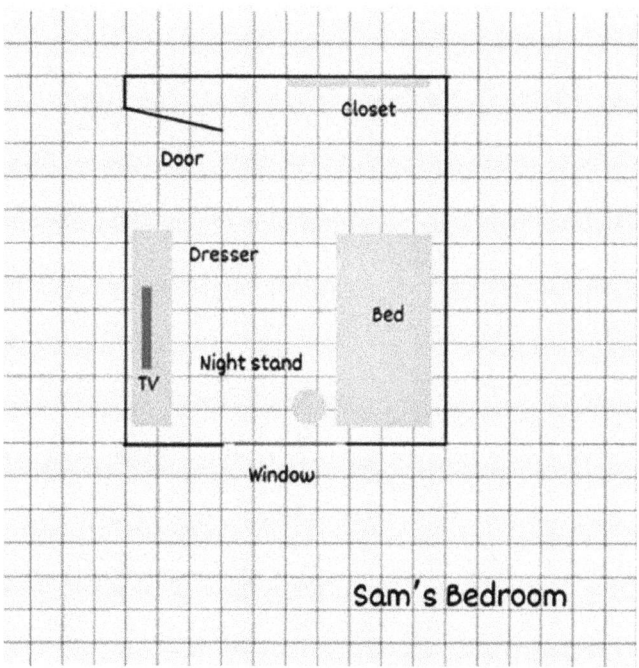

Vacation Plan

Getting ready for vacation takes time and planning. Check off items as you gather and pack them. You can copy and paste this list to your computer to create a custom plan.

Travel documents

- Airline tickets
- Passports, Visas, etc.
- Hotel reservations
- Car rental

First Aid

- Sunscreen
- Bug spray
- Topical anti-itch
- Topical antibacterial
- Q-tips
- Band-aids

Comfort

- Food
- Drinks
- Books
- Magazines

Electronics

- Cell phones
- Computers
- Tablets
- Chargers
- Passwords
- Camera

Small children

- Bottles
- Food & formula
- Snacks
- Items for sleep

- Car seat
- Stroller
- Diapers
- Entertainment
- Toys
- Blankets & pillows

Pets

- Travel documents
- Vet & shot records
- Food for each day
- Meds for each day
- Flea & tick
- Towels & shampoo
- Grooming supplies
- Crates
- Leashes & harnesses

Clothing & shoes for each traveler

- Shirts
- Pants
- Jeans
- Shorts
- Formal attire
- Under garments
- Socks
- Sleep attire

- Outerwear
- Sandals
- Formal shoes
- Athletic
- Hiking, golf, etc
- Boots

Toiletries for each traveler

- Make-up
- Deodorant
- Shampoo
- Conditioner
- Hair care
- Shave cream
- Perfume
- Cologne
- Razor

Medications for each traveler

- Daily medications
- Daily supplements

Vacation Pet Care Plan

If you have pets, a care plan for them is essential. You may have a family emergency, a business trip, or a planned vacation at a location that doesn't allow pets. You will have peace of mind knowing your pet's specific plan is being followed. In addition, you can email the plan to a caregiver if you are called out on a family emergency. Create a document and include the following information:

- Pet names, breeds, ages
- Pet sitter contact information
- Pet owner contact information
- Vet information
- Vet hospital information
- Daycare facility information
- Dates of care
- Time care begins
- Time care ends
- Daily feeding routine – amount and times of day
- Daily exercise routine – amount and times of day
- Daily medication routine – amount and times of day
- Specific details

Home Improvement Project Summary

Use a 3-ring binder to create a record of your home improvement projects. This will help you track the money you have invested in your home. When it is time to sell your home, you will have a valuable record to provide realtors and potential buyers.

For each project, include any of the following information that is relevant to your project:

- Name of project
- Date completed
- Cost
- Contractor name
- Contractor address

- Contractor phone
- Would you use the contractor again?
- How would you rate the quality of workmanship?
- Paint brand
- Paint color
- Finish (flat, matte, semi)
- Lighting brand
- Lighting product number
- Flooring brand
- Flooring color
- Flooring type
- Flooring grout color, product number
- Countertop brand
- Countertop product number
- Toilet brand
- Toilet product number
- Sink brand
- Sink product number
- Additional information

Home Maintenance

Keep track of your home's care and repairs. You will have all the important information ready when you need additional service and a valuable record when you sell your home. You can add these records to the 3-ring binder you created for Home Improvement Projects.

- Name of project/service
- Date completed
- Cost
- Contractor name
- Contractor address
- Contractor phone
- Contractor website
- Contract signed? Yes or No
- Are you happy with the workmanship?
- Warranty? Yes or No

Chapter Eleven

DOWNSIZING

Strategically Scaling Back

Decluttering means removing unwanted or unnecessary items that do not hold special value. When you are downsizing, you are often faced with getting rid of items you may still enjoy but do not have the space to keep. If you declutter first, you will likely reduce the need to downsize. This plan is designed to help you reduce unwanted and unnecessary items before you begin evaluating items that hold special value.

By shifting your mindset about your belongings, it is easier to part with unnecessary things. If items are treated as inventory with a purpose rather than treasure, you can part with items that do not serve a purpose or are unused excess. This creates space for the most important things you own. If you are a family member helping an older adult, try your best to be patient. Some individuals may need more time to make decisions.

Reducing your household inventory offers these benefits:

- Your home will stay neat and organized if your personal items are neatly stored.

- You can quickly find what you're looking without stress.

- You will spend less time cleaning up, organizing, and putting things away.

- You will save money on movers and packing materials when you move.

- You will save money when shopping if you buy only what you need and reduce food waste. The cost of groceries has increased substantially recently.

- You will need less space, which could save money if you move to a smaller home.

- You will enjoy more open space, making your home feel larger.

- You will save on storage fees. The fees can quickly surpass the value of the stored items.

Personal Items vs. Household Inventory

Most of us enjoy new things. However, if we never unload the old, worn-out items, our homes quickly fill up with clutter. By switching your mindset about personal and household items, you can eliminate excess more quickly and without a sense of loss. For instance, do you need old magazines? Do you read them? *Are these items serving a purpose?*

Start decluttering by first removing low-value items. These items do not hold special meaning. While it may be easy for you to make decisions about these things, working on just one item at a time will minimize your loved one's stress and confusion. You can also create clear and separate stacks of magazines, newspapers, and expired food. The amount of storage room needed for low-value household inventory will become evident. Remember, you will need patience while managing your loved one's mental and emotional state throughout the process.

Low-Value Household Inventory: Recycle or Trash

- Old newspapers
- Old magazines
- Old files
- Expired food
- Old office supplies
- Old cleaning supplies
- Damaged home goods
- Damaged home decor
- Damaged clothing

Medium Value Household Inventory: Donate or Sell

- Movies
- Music
- Books
- Gently used home goods
- Gently used decor
- Most furniture
- Kitchen items
- Small appliances
- Yard equipment
- Tools

High-Value Items: Personal and Household Items

High-value items have either sentimental or monetary value. This is the most difficult category to sort. Many individuals will have a difficult time parting with things they value. If you are helping someone downsize, set these items aside and respect the value they hold. Clearly label any items the owner wishes to save and set them aside in a separate room if possible. If the original owner has died, allow family members time to choose items they wish to keep if these items are not already defined by a Last Will and Testament.

Take breaks! Downsizing is mentally, emotionally, and physically exhausting work. Possessions often bring back a lifetime of priceless memories. Also, consider that some antiques could be quite valuable. Try not to rush through things.

If you plan to sell items, check local listings for similar items. Too often, used furniture doesn't hold its value well unless it is an antique. Complete the Donation Plan Worksheet before you begin. Use the worksheets in Chapter Ten to assist you in organizing and downsizing specific rooms, such as the kitchen or bedroom.

Downsizing an individual with dementia is very challenging. The disease makes it difficult for him or her to understand what is valuable and what is unnecessary clutter. You should anticipate having lengthy discussions about old magazines or other items that most of us would easily throw away or recycle. The old worn-out saying "one man's trash is another man's treasure" will play out in front of you over and over. Sorting and organizing for a parent is difficult because they often covet their treasures. My mother has dementia. Downsizing and removing excess items was frustrating, stressful, and painful. Keep in mind your loved one's future health needs and safety.

Caregiver Legal and Financial Management

Caring for a senior parent or other family member often means assuming many roles. You might help with meals, doctor appointments, household chores, and more. You may eventually become a Power of Attorney, making financial and medical decisions on behalf of your loved one. You will likely pay monthly bills as a POA. Having all important documents ready for financial management and medical emergencies allows you to focus on your loved one rather than searching for lost documents. You could keep documents in a file or a 3-ring binder. If you are using a binder, consider storing pages in sheet protectors.

Professional Legal and Financial Help

Since laws vary from one location to the next, it is best to work with reputable local financial planners to manage financial assets. Also, be sure to consult with an Estate Planning Attorney to complete the necessary documents for the ongoing care and eventual death of your family member. Be sure you know how financial assets and physical property will be handled before the senior's mental or physical health declines. This includes meeting with bankers to assign beneficiaries at each institution. If you gather all of your records before meeting with an Estate Planner, the professional will be better equipped to guide you through the process.

Below is a list of common information you will need to have readily available. All situations are unique. Many of the professionals will need a copy of your POA documents.

Important Contacts

Assisted living facility

- Contact name

- Address
- Phone
- Website

Primary Physician

- Address
- Phone
- Website

Legal firm name

- Attorney
- Address
- Phone
- Website

Financial Advisor/Planner Firm

- Planner
- Name
- Address
- Phone
- Website

Important Documents:

- Driver's license or ID card
- Social Security card and documents
- Birth certificate
- Medical insurance ID cards

- Medicare card
- Medicaid card
- Medical Power of Attorney document
- Financial Power of Attorney document
- Living will
- Last Will and Testament
- Burial plan
- Funeral plan
- Life insurance policies
- Bank accounts
- Retirement/financial accounts
- Current address
- Old address
- Monthly bills

Be sure to provide your mailing address to each company, institution, government office, and the United States Postal Service.

Chapter Twelve

HOUSEHOLD MOVING WORKSHEETS

Overview

One of the biggest challenges in making a household move easier is getting organized and thinking through all of the steps that need to be done. This overview provides a brief description of each step you will need to complete to accomplish the goal of moving. Each step outlined below has its own worksheet in this chapter. As with the Home Organization portion of this book, jump in and complete the tasks in the order that makes the most sense to you. You may find having a 3-ring binder labeled "Moving" is very helpful. There are many steps to complete before, during, and after your move.

Step 1: Declutter. If you have time to plan ahead, reducing your household inventory is the most important first step in your moving journey. You can toss one box of unused items into a car or moving truck and place it on a shelf with little effort. However, most of us have far more than one box of unused items. For each box, there is a cost associated. You must pay to box it, move it onto a truck, pay for transportation, move it off the truck, and then pay for the space to store it in your new home. Every residence offers a specific number of square feet. If your storage needs exceed your available space, you will have the added expense of a storage unit. The unused items create clutter, work, and expenses. Consider the boxes, tape, packing paper, bubble wrap, and labor involved in moving five boxes of unused magazines or books, for instance.

Step 2: Room Planning. Sometimes, our current home isn't ideally organized. We may have items scattered throughout our home rather than grouped and stored where they are used. You know which areas of your home function well and which areas need improvement. Use that information to make a plan for your new home. Maybe you are constantly battling your children about getting homework completed because they procrastinate and need better supervision. Working in the kitchen instead of their bedrooms might be a solution. Maybe you want to read while your spouse would like to watch TV in the evening. You will need different locations for these activities. Use the Room Planning Worksheet to make those adjustments. Then pack according to the room uses, placing items where they will be used. This is a very important step. If the items are not where they are used, one person must either constantly move things around in the home or battle with family members to put things away. This also leads to more lost items. "Have you seen my.." "Where did you use it last?" When your items are easy to find, easy to use, and easy to put away, your entire home will feel clutter-free.

Step 3: Temporary Storage. You may find it useful to use companies like Pods.com to store items you do not frequently use. Plan ahead and reserve storage containers and storage units.

This eliminates the need to move every box into your new home immediately.

Step 4: Change of Address. Many businesses and government offices allow you to change your address online. The Change of Address Worksheet provides an outline of the places you will need to contact.

Step 5: Hire a Moving Company. Complete this step in advance so you can research companies. Some may charge by the job, while others may charge hourly. Many companies have a minimum charge. Check with coworkers, friends, and family, and read online reviews. Get several estimates and hire a company ahead of time to reserve your move date. Also, consider whether or not they will be moving boxes or just heavy furniture. Will you rent a truck as well? What method works for your budget, time, and energy?

Step 6: Packing for You and Your Family. Even the most organized residential move is stressful. Be sure to have the things you need set aside so you can bathe and change clothes without searching through piles of boxes.

Step 7: Purchase Moving Supplies. Check office supply stores and big box stores for moving boxes and tape. Also, consider reusable fabric totes that can be used to store clothing or bedding long-term in your home. The totes would allow you to move the items and place them on the shelf without unpacking. They also provide a neat way to store things on higher shelves.

Step 8: Staging Your Home. If you are selling your home, it needs to visually sell itself. Use the Staging Your Home Worksheet to get your home ready for guests. Staging does not need to be costly. Simple efforts, such as setting the table, cleaning, and placing fresh flowers or fresh fruit on the countertop, can make your house feel more welcoming. Remember, buyers are buying a lifestyle. What is it like to live here? Can they see themselves calling your house their home?

Step 9: Packing Household Items. Having a plan of attack will help you keep this process organized. Many of your things will be in boxes for several weeks or longer.

Step 10: Unpacking. Unpack your suitcases first to have access to toiletries and clothing. Decide where you want to store valuable items and important papers while your home is full of boxes, bubble wrap, etc. Next, use your Room Planning Worksheets to place furniture throughout your home. Unpack your fragile items after you unpack all other items to prevent damage. Lastly, evaluate your storage needs in each room.

Temporary Storage

Plan ahead and reserve storage containers and/or storage units. Service providers such as Pods.com will allow you to pack a storage container that will be left in your current residential driveway for a period of time. They will then move the storage container to your new residence and pick up the empty unit at a later date. I used Pods.com when we moved and had a great experience. We placed our lawn tractor, outdoor furniture, seasonal items, and many boxes in the unit.

You can also use other temporary storage. If you need to remove some items from your home for showings and do not want a storage container in your driveway, check your area for temporary storage. Your home will be less cluttered for showings, and your moving day will be focused on the more important items. Be sure to get more than one estimate.

Temporary Storage Facility:

- Name
- Address
- Phone
- Website
- Start date
- End date
- Initial fee
- Gate code
- Monthly fee

Helpful Hint: Short-term temporary storage can be a valuable piece of the moving puzzle. Try to set a limit on how long you will use the facility. The fees can add up quickly.

Change of Address

Before you move, contact each of the following businesses, government offices, and your personal contacts. Provide an effective date and your new address. You may be able to do some of this online. Some financial and government offices may want you to make the change in person. If you are moving out of the area, be sure to make changing your address a priority. The UPS Store may have mailboxes you can rent temporarily if the need arises. For friends and family, it may help them if you list both your new and old address on a postcard especially if they live out of state or are older.

Child Care

- Babysitter
- Daycare
- Nanny

Financial

- Accountant
- Banks/bank accounts
- Credit cards
- Savings accounts
- 401k
- Annuities
- Investment accounts

Government

- Post office
- Passport
- Driver's license
- Voter Registration

Home

- Mortgage
- Home/renter
- Insurance storage facility
- Home security
- Utilities

Medical

- Doctors
- Specialists
- Hospitals
- Dental
- Eye

Personal

- Friends
- Family
- Work

Pets

- Daycare
- Dog sitter
- Veterinarians
- Vet hospital

Retail Local & Online

- Billing addresses
- Shipping addresses

Schools

- Preschool
- Elementary
- Middle school
- High school
- College/university

Services

- Cell phone
- Internet provider
- Cable/satellite

Subscriptions

- Newspapers
- Magazines

Any Additional Companies

Moving Companies

Movers must be reliable, careful, and ready to work. Be sure to read online reviews. Did the company's customers state they were on time and worked diligently? Will you be billed by the hour or by the job? If you are billed hourly, you will likely be billed for travel time starting from when the workers leave their company until they return. Be sure to get several estimates. Collect the same information for each company so you can compare them side by side. A company that charges by the hour might be less expensive for a small job rather than a company that has a minimum 1/2 day rate. However, that small job can become expensive with the wrong company. If you try to save time by not doing enough research, moving day might become very costly and frustrating. If the movers do a great job, consider tipping them.

Moving Company Estimates

1. Name
2. Address
3. Phone
4. Website
5. Start date
6. Hourly fee
7. Job rate fee
8. Additional notes

Packing for You and Your Family

Before you begin packing for your move, think about the items you use daily and set those items aside. Pack a suitcase for each family member as if you are going on a five-day vacation. Be sure to pack for your pets as well. You will have countless boxes stacked all over your new home, and you will be tired and frustrated. This is a nearly unavoidable part of the moving process. If you place clothing and personal items in a suitcase in your personal vehicle, you will be able to get dressed and care for pets until things are put away in your new home. You can use the Vacation Plan Worksheet for a more comprehensive list.

Packing List

- Shirts
- Pants
- Shoes
- Socks
- Undergarments
- Shampoo
- Conditioner
- Hair spray
- Hair dryer
- Make-up
- Deodorant
- Toilet paper
- Towels
- Soap
- Toothbrush

- Toothpaste
- Cell phone
- Cell phone charger
- Personal electronic devices
- Medications
- Vitamins
- Work documents
- Work supplies
- School work
- School supplies
- Important papers
- Valuables such as jewelry
- Pet leashes
- Pet bowls
- Pet food
- Pet medications

Helpful Hint: Your pets may be very stressed during a household move. If daycare is an option, it might be best if your pets spend the day safely offsite.

Before and after the big moving day, be sure to photograph every room of your home. You may need to verify your home's condition.

Moving Supplies

More than likely, most of your moving supplies will be recycled or thrown away. Try to save money on most of your supplies by comparing local and online store prices. However, spend the extra money on items that will save you time and energy, such as color-coded moving label stickers. They are available on Amazon.com.

Think about how nice it will be at the end of a long day to stack boxes by color rather than reading every label. Plus, if a box ends up misplaced, it will stand out if the label is red in a stack of green labels.

Free boxes could be cost effective, but they also might be a disaster. If you pick up boxes at a cardboard donation site, they might have unwanted pests like bed bugs. Retailer shipping boxes might be a safe option. Be sure to check with the store's management before helping yourself to boxes.

Shopping List

- Boxes
- Bubble wrap
- Packing paper
- Packing tape
- Packing tape dispenser
- Scissors
- Sharpies
- Color-coded moving label stickers
- Fragile stickers

Suppliers to Consider

- Home Depot
- Lowes
- U Haul
- Moving companies
- Walmart
- Amazon.com
- Office supply stores
- Local retailers

Staging Your Home

Make A Memorable First Impression!

The goal of staging your home is to make your home more attractive to potential buyers. If you have more potential buyers interested, you may receive more and possibly higher offers. Staging your home before photographs, open houses, and showings helps potential buyers see themselves living in your home.

Since your online home listing includes photographs, it will be obvious if your home has been well cared for or neglected. If buyers need to spend time and money on countless updates, they may not attend a showing. If your home is well-maintained but cluttered, you may lose potential buyers as well. When you are looking at homes, what stands out to you? What makes a home feel warm and inviting? This worksheet will help you get your home ready for sale, step by step, room by room. Be sure to make notes as you go through your home.

Go through each point and decide what work you would like to complete to stage your home.

- **Cleaning makes a difference.** You will not provide a great first impression if potential buyers see pet hair, dirty clothes, dust, dirty floors, and or dirty carpeting. Consider professional cleaners if you need help.

- **Room layout makes a difference.** Crowded rooms and empty rooms can make it difficult for buyers to see the size of the room. Store excess furniture and accessories in short-term storage if necessary. Use the Room Planning Worksheet if your room layouts need revisiting.

- **Get rid of excess.** If you have clutter, your home may look like it lacks adequate storage. In addition, moving one box of unwanted items is manageable. Moving 30 boxes will not only increase the cost of your move, but it will increase your work and frustration. Most importantly, you will decrease the space in your new home. Try to avoid stocking up on food and other items until after your move.

- **ROI.** There is no way to calculate an exact return on investment for any home improvement project. Work within your budget and try to make the most impact.

- **Outdoor Appearance.** Your home's first impression is usually the front of your house. Potential buyers may drive by listings before they decide to go to showings. Trim shrubs, pull weeds, edge and mulch beds, mow the lawn, edge paved areas, plant annuals, and remove debris. Power wash the house, deck or paved areas. Add new pillows to outdoor seating.

- **Foyer.** This area is important since it will provide the first impression of your home's interior. Is it warm, inviting, and clean? Does it smell clean and fresh? Avoid heavy air fresheners.

- **Kitchen.** Kitchens are all about storage and workspace. Try to avoid having small appliances and kitchen utensils on the counters. It makes the room look cluttered. It also conveys the storage is inadequate.

- **Closets.** Too many items in a closet can make it look small and inefficient. Place out-of-season clothing and other items that are rarely used in storage instead of adding additional shelves to closets.

- **Bedrooms.** New paint and bedding can give bedrooms a fresh, clean appearance.

- **Bathrooms.** Bathrooms can look noticeably out of date. Painting cabinets and replacing dated hardware is relatively inexpensive. Also, consider painting the walls.

You could also replace the light fixture or just replace the light globes. Don't forget to update the old switch plates. Choose neutral colors. Beige is easy for most people to live with until they can make it their own. Add new towels and soap dishes. Full bathroom remodels are very expensive and may deter new owners. Try to make your bathrooms look fresh without a huge investment.

- **Storage.** If you need to add basement shelving, consider heavy grade plastic shelving kits that can be easily torn down. They are lightweight and easy to move and store when not in use. These units are a great, inexpensive investment and can be found online and at home improvement centers.

- **Best Feature.** Every home is unique. Is there a specific area inside or outside your home that sets it apart? Is it memorable in a good way? Can you make it a featured area by adding decor?

- **Updates.** Create a home improvement binder or file. Include receipts and work orders. It can be shown to the realtors and/or given to the new homeowner if you do not need the records. Simply insert receipts and work orders of completed updates into sheet protectors. Potential buyers will see that you have invested in the property and taken good care of it.

Go Digital

Photograph each one of your rooms in its current state. How does each area look? Ask your realtor for guidance. Also, ask friends or family for their opinion. Simply changing artwork, adding pillows, or changing curtains can make a big impact. You are trying to sell your home for the most value. Ask your listing agent for recommendations and look online for ideas. Use the things you already have if possible. If you buy new items, make sure you can use and enjoy them in your new home.

Create a Budget

There is no way to know an exact return on a specific home improvement project. However, there are many resources to give you an approximate idea. Painting walls and adding new area rugs can improve the overall appearance of a room without costing a great deal. Adding colorful throw pillows is fairly inexpensive but adds visual interest. If you don't stage your home, it could stay on the market longer or attract fewer potential buyers. Work within your budget but show some attention to details, even if it is just a thorough cleaning. Buyers need to see themselves living in your house and enjoying it rather than looking at all the work that needs to be completed.

Helpful Hint: You are selling a lifestyle. *Think about how you feel looking at potential new homes. How will buyers feel about living in your home?*

Packing Household Items

While you could just start boxing things in preparation for your move, having a plan will make the entire process less stressful. There will be times when you cannot find items, no matter how well you have prepared. However, you can minimize the frustration if you have essential items ready for use.

Step 1: Set aside daily use items for use during your move.

Step 2: Valuable items and important papers need special care. Do not leave these items for the movers. Is it possible to store these items at a trusted family member's house? If not, place them in your personal vehicle on moving day before the moving company arrives. When you are packing, mark the boxes well and set the boxes with your suitcases. Temporary storage could be broken into so do not trust these items to those locations.

Step 3: Next, start packing items for temporary storage. These items could include holiday decorations, out-of-season clothing, lawn care equipment, and sporting goods. If you use Pods.com or a similar company, the items will be in your driveway for easy access should you realize you need them sooner rather than later. Be sure to label boxes by room. Sorting boxes by color will be easier for you and your movers. If a box is misplaced, it will be easy to spot. Color-coded moving labels can be found on Amazon.com.

Step 4: After you have completed packing for temporary storage, begin packing the remaining items from each room. Be sure to label each box well. This might be time-consuming now, but it will pay off in a big way when you have stacks of boxes in every room. Mark fragile items well. You can purchase fragile stickers at office supply stores and on Amazon. Writing "FRAGILE" on the box with a Sharpie isn't as noticeable as a red label. It is also faster to apply several stickers to the box.

Step 5: Label the items you need right away with "OPEN FIRST" so you can make separate stacks on moving day. Even if you do not use a temporary storage facility, your items will be boxed for a period of time. You can put your pressure cooker away later, but you will need clean lines to make beds.

Step 6: Take breaks. Try to stay focused while you are packing. You are likely to find things you don't want or need that can be thrown away or donated. Every box creates added expensive, added labor and added clutter in your new home.

Unpacking

Easy to find, easy to use, easy to put away.

Step 1: If you have the time before your movers arrive, thoroughly clean your new home before you begin putting things away. You could hire a company to do this work for you. Also, try to have rooms painted.

Step 2: Unpack your suitcases. Having easy access to your essential items will reduce your stress. Keep all of your daily use items away from the other boxes.

Step 3: Store important papers and valuables in a bedroom closet or another low-traffic area if you are unable to keep them off-site. Put these away once most of the house is unpacked and organized.

Step 4: After the furniture is placed, begin bringing in the boxes and placing them in their assigned rooms. If you simply pile everything in one room, you will have the task of moving the boxes twice. What if you forgot to set aside bath towels, and the linen closet box is lost somewhere in that massive pile? You will be tired, frustrated, stressed, and unable to take a hot shower.

Step 5: Unpack and put away "OPEN FIRST" items. Then, unpack daily use items such as clothing, kitchen items, and bathroom items. Next, unpack entertainment items. If possible, save fragile items for last. As you are putting things away, pull out any remaining items you don't want or need. If possible, reuse or recycle boxes.

Step 6: Rest and enjoy your new home! Greet your neighbors. Find a new restaurant. Have a picnic in the backyard. The remaining boxes will be there in the morning.

Step 7: After you settle into your new home, evaluate the storage in each room. Find storage that is functional first and beautiful second. **Items are perfectly put away if they are easy to find, easy to use, and easy to put away.** After you have taken time to rest, address storage needs in each room. You may need additional storage to accommodate the items used in each room. Make sure your storage is highly functional and versatile.

Welcome Home!

Conclusion

It's About Time

I magine looking back and reminiscing about a day spent at the beach with your loved ones. Will you remember the peaceful sound of waves crashing against the shore as you watched your children build sand castles? Perhaps one of your favorite memories will be that lazy day you spent with your family enjoying a picnic under a majestic shade tree in a national park. You need to deliberately create time for yourself and your loved ones to create these moments. Your parents will age, and your children move away. We all run out of time as life changes.

As you long for those moments that make you feel alive and connected, busy schedules often get in the way. We put off spending time meaningfully to handle the latest urgent set of tasks. Household chores may be unavoidable, but with a better organization and increased efficiency, you can reclaim your life. By decluttering and organizing your home, you not only free up living space, you also free up time and energy on chores and daily straightening. Your family can find, use, and put away items without you. They can learn to be more organized and efficient.

You will have fewer battles over routine tasks such as completing homework if you create the right workspace. Overall, organization creates a more peaceful environment where your entire family can truly unwind and spend quality time together.

Remember, life is meant to be enjoyed. Take the time to appreciate the beauty of the world around you, indulge in new experiences, and nurture the relationships that bring you happiness and fulfillment. Your time is precious, so make sure you use it in a way that fills your soul and leaves you with unforgettable memories.

Find Your Passion

Meet Daisy, our newest family member. She was rescued and retired from breeding a couple of years ago. I find tremendous meaning and joy in providing a loving home to rescue dogs. While I would love to take in countless dogs, I choose to dedicate my free time to enjoying art and supporting pets instead. I recently created a new website, www.APetsLifeinArt.com, to offer custom pet portraits. I donate a portion of the sales to animal shelters.

Someday, I plan to turn my love of horses into another life-saving mission through art and rescue.

What brings purpose to your life? Your life as a caregiver will eventually change. If you are like me and have spent countless years dedicating yourself to caring for everyone else's needs, it may take time for you to decide what your next chapter looks like. It took time for me to reconnect with myself. However, I am finally able to enjoy art, nature, and animals once again. You are far more than a caregiver. Find your passion!

Best wishes,

Rebecca Hartman

www.ingramcontent.com/pod-product-compliance
Lightning Source LLC
Chambersburg PA
CBHW051535120626
46551CB00012B/1240